Win Win or Else

CORWIN
PRESS

The Corwin Press logo—a raven striding across an open book—represents the happy union of courage and learning. We are a professional-level publisher of books and journals for K–12 educators, and we are committed to creating and providing resources that embody these qualities. Corwin's motto is "Success for All Learners."

Win Win or Else

or Else

Collective Bargaining in an Age of Public Discontent

William G. Keane

CORWIN PRESS, INC.
A Sage Publications Company
Thousand Oaks, California

For information address:

Corwin Press, Inc.
A Sage Publications Company
2455 Teller Road
Thousand Oaks, California 91320
e-mail: order@corwin.sagepub.com

SAGE Publications Ltd.
6 Bonhill Street
London EC2A 4PU
United Kingdom

SAGE Publications India Pvt. Ltd.
M-32 Market
Greater Kailash I
New Delhi 110 048 India

Printed in the United States of America

Library of Congress Cataloging-in-Publication Data

Keane, William G.
    Win/win or else : collective bargaining in an age of public
discontent / William G. Keane.
        p.   cm.
    Includes bibliographical references.
    ISBN 0-8039-6424-2 (cloth : alk. paper). — ISBN 0-8039-6319-X
(pbk. : alk. paper)
        1. Collective bargaining—Teachers—United States. 2. Teachers'
unions—United States. I. Title.
LB2844.59.U6K43   1996
331.89'041—dc20   95-42476

This book is printed on acid-free paper.

96 97 98 99 00 10 9 8 7 6 5 4 3 2 1

Corwin Press Production Editor: S. Marlene Head

Contents

Acknowledgments   vii

About the Author   viii

Introduction   1

1 Collective Bargaining: Past and Present   4
    • Why the Bargaining Table Has Pointed Edges
    • Collective Bargaining Tomorrow: Making the
    Square Table Round • Have the Purposes of
    Collective Bargaining Changed? • The Need
    for Partnership • Summary

2 Preparing for Negotiations   13
    • Developing a Partnership: Defining Roles and
    Learning Skills • Learning to Work Together
    • Summary

3 The Bargaining Process: Less Is More   23
    • Starting With Beliefs and First Principles
    • Managing Meetings • Working Together
    • Getting to a Contract • Summary

4 Managing Conflict   36
    • Resolving Conflicts: A General Perspective
    • Conflicts Over Interests • Conflicts Over
    Existing Contracts • Summary

5 Collective Bargaining in the Future   47
    • Will Unions and Bargaining Disappear? • Will
    Union-Board Relationships Change? • Changing
    Roles, Changing Relationships • Getting Started
    • Summary

Resource A: Win/Win Bargaining:
A Practitioner's Checklist   59

Glossary   62

Annotated Bibliography, Other Suggested
Readings, and References   65

Acknowledgments

This book was written to help practitioners of the collective bargaining process reach agreements more effectively and efficiently. Theories presented in the text have, in one context or another, proven successful at the table. Several educators have helped assure the reality of the theory.

Dr. Jerry J. Herman, Professor of Education in the Department of Administration and Policy at the University of Alabama, identified the need for more detailed treatment of collaborative bargaining than is readily available. The importance of his encouragement and support cannot be minimized.

Appreciation for help in seeing the application of theory to practice is due to Duane Lewis, Assistant Superintendent for Personnel Services in the Clarkston (MI) Community Schools; Dr. Edward Callahan, Executive Director of Human Resources, Oakland (MI) Community College; Raymond Wolf, Director of Personnel for the Ferndale (MI) School District; and Michael P. Long, J.D., Associate Professor and Coordinator of the Labor Studies Program at Oakland University (MI).

Special thanks for technical assistance in preparing the manuscript for publication are due to my colleague, Dr. James F. Cipielewski, and my son, Kevin Keane.

My wife, Gerry, always believed in the project, even when I wavered.

About the Author

William G. Keane served for 23 years as a public school superintendent. During the first 9 years of that period, he served as the chief executive of the Berkley Public Schools in Berkley, Michigan. From 1980 to 1994, he was superintendent of Oakland Schools, a service agency serving 28 local school districts and 170,000 public school students in Oakland County, Michigan. Prior to the superintendencies, he served as a junior high school and high school English teacher in New York, a director of secondary education in Michigan, and assistant superintendent of curriculum and instruction for the Woodbridge, New Jersey, public schools. He is now associate professor in the Department of Curriculum, Instruction, and Leadership at Oakland University in Rochester, Michigan.

During the past 20 years, he has served as an adjunct instructor at Eastern Michigan University, Wayne State University, Northern Michigan University, and for 3 years at Oakland University before joining their faculty full time in 1994. He also serves as director for the Education Specialist program in addition to his teaching duties. His areas of focus have been school personnel administration and collective bargaining. His articles and book reviews have appeared in *The American School Board Journal*, *The School Administrator*, and other magazines and professional journals.

Dr. Keane has a B.A. in English from St. John's University (New York), an M.A. in English from Columbia University, and an Ed.D. in curriculum and administration from Teachers College, Columbia University.

Introduction

Twenty-five years ago, readers of Alvin Toffler's *Future Shock* often responded with an intellectual affirmation of the accelerating pace of social change that was described in the book. Today's readers now experience viscerally the dizzying pace of change in everything about their lives. The title of a theatrical production of the same time period, *Stop the World: I Want to Get Off*, describes an emotional response that most individuals have had ever more frequently.

The impact of technology on information access, the development of a global economy, the changes in the geopolitical structure governing international relationships, the growing polarization of American politics, the evolution of the American population to a majority of minorities, and the changing roles of men and women in families and in society all seem to affect everyone in some way or other. A "brave new world" is no longer on the horizon. It is here.

Even within the microworld of public education, the rate of change is accelerating. Private businesses, such as the Edison Project and Education Alternatives Inc. (EAI), are competing for the right to serve public education students. Milwaukee has a small voucher program. Chicago has dramatically changed the governance structure of public education, placing significant decision-making power at the building level. New York City is developing, with the support of the teacher union, a series of minischools run

1

outside the school bureaucracy insofar as possible. By mid-1995, 19 states had passed legislation permitting charter schools, and 20 more were considering such legislation. In some states, charter schools are largely independent of the bureaucratic control of school boards in most respects.

In the future, the conservative drift of political opinion in the United States may have an even more fundamental impact on public education in general and on collective bargaining specifically. Initiatives have been passed in some states to deny teachers automatic access to "fair share" fees charged to nonunion teachers for bargaining services. Indiana is one example. In other states, "right to work" initiatives are on the horizon. Such legislation would eliminate automatic dues deductions for unions. Without the authority to require the payment of dues, teacher unions would be seriously wounded and their power at the bargaining table noticeably eroded. Efforts to impose severe financial penalties against teacher unions for calling a strike are beginning to surface.

Collective bargaining in education, drawn from an industrial model, is facing environmental changes that will challenge the continuation of this system and the present teacher union structure that enables it to operate. This really should be no surprise. Unions have had a hard time in the private industrial sector for a long time. After reaching a peak in 1953, unions in the private sector have been a declining presence ever since. Brain workers cannot be organized as easily as those who work with their hands. The need for information workers is growing rapidly; more and more durable goods are being produced by fewer and fewer people.

School boards, the public's direct representatives, are also being subjected to a louder and louder chorus of censure. Studies such as those conducted by the Twentieth Century Fund and the Institute for Educational Leadership have suggested that school boards as we know them should be abolished or at least fundamentally restructured.

It is within the context of this maelstrom of change that this book attempts to suggest how collective bargaining needs to adapt to a new environment. The fundamental requirement for successful win/win bargaining is both mutual trust and mutual need. Noisy collective bargaining conflicts and angry teacher strikes clearly are no longer in anyone's interest. The very survival of public education may, to a significant extent, depend on the ability of teachers, school boards, and parents to decide together how to use scarce resources for maximum benefit and share power to the satisfaction of all.

The late Irving Goldaber (1982) may have been the first to coin the term *win/win bargaining*. He described it as a process in which both parties seek solutions that will permit each side to achieve its goals. All other kinds of bargaining—win/lose and lose/lose—are self-defeating because losing parties are always focused on recapturing what was lost, rather than problem solving, the next time a contract must be negotiated.

Win/win bargaining has been described by different names, all focused on the same concept. The terms *collaborative bargaining, mutual gaining,* and *principled bargaining* have been used in the literature. In this book, the term *cooperative bargaining* is used in the hope of avoiding the allegations of some that "collaborative bargaining" implies the need to forgo genuine interests as the price of goodwill at the table.

1

Collective Bargaining:
Past and Present

Books continue to flow from the presses advising school boards and administrators how to "win" at the game of collective bargaining. The copyright dates are irrelevant for many of them. They are written as though the authors lived in a time warp. The advice is the same whether the book is written for a 1975 or a 1995 audience: Here's how to get the advantage, confuse the opposition, manipulate the public and the press, and so forth. *This* is not one of those publications.

Collective bargaining for educators is almost certainly entering a very different era. The economic, political, and social contexts in which American public education will operate in the future are unlikely to be anything like the environment of the past 30 years. As an artifact of the present educational system, collective bargaining will have to change with the system itself or become a useless and irrelevant appendage.

Why the Bargaining Table Has Pointed Edges

The Beginnings of Collective Bargaining

Collective bargaining is a legitimate vehicle for solving problems. Whether approached from an old-fashioned adversarial model or a modern cooperative prototype, problems did and still do get resolved in a process that requires both sides to be attentive to each other's concerns.

Prior to collective bargaining, the employer, who owned all the resources, shared them with workers only insofar as conscience required or circumstance permitted. Workers could be paid a pittance if the employer controlled the labor market and no other employer was competing for scarce workers. Collective bargaining, given its most important stimulus through the federal Wagner Act of 1935, *required* employers to discuss matters of compensation and working conditions with representatives selected by employees. No longer were workers and unions suppliants. They had the right to bargain, not request. They were powerful in their own right.

Workers entered this new process largely with the conviction that private employers had previously shared wealth unfairly. Owners and managers got the lion's share of profits. Workers got the leavings. There was no reason to believe that employers would voluntarily give workers a larger share of the pie through collective bargaining. If the workers were to gain a decent wage and humane working conditions, such improvements would have to be forcibly extracted from employers. The bloody battles between ownership of the Ford Motor Car Company and the United Automobile Workers (UAW) in the late 1930s formed a historical precedent that affected the mindset of union leaders for generations.

Private sector employers also had reasons to enter into collective bargaining with trepidation. Managers had been schooled through the work of writers such as Frederick W. Taylor (1911) to believe that it was the way workers were organized to do work, not the feelings or attitudes or ideas of workers, that made a difference in productivity. To be successful, managers needed an almost unfettered right to design work and assign workers. In fact, most managers thought of workers with a mental model that years later Douglas McGregor (1960) made famous as Theory X: a belief that workers are inherently lazy, unambitious, and resistant to change. An employer coming to the bargaining table with that mind-set about the motivations of workers is understandably coming reluctantly. Worker proposals, almost by definition, are going to be viewed as self-serving, crafted to require less work for more money.

Some of the language of traditional collective bargaining suggests its roots. Employees do not identify problems and concerns; they make "demands" on the employer. Why demands? Why "take-aways"? Because prior to collective bargaining, employees had, at best, the right as individuals to request improvements in compensation and working conditions. Now they were "equals." They had strength in their mutual resolve. They would be respected. They would be heard.

Collective Bargaining in Education

Collective bargaining for teachers made its first impact in the 1960s. After President John F. Kennedy signed an executive order in 1962 permitting collective bargaining for federal public employees, though prohibiting strikes, the door was opened for state legislators, prodded by effective organizing and lobbying efforts by the National Education Association (NEA) and the American Federation of Teachers (AFT), to pass legislation permitting teachers and school boards to bargain collectively. Wisconsin implemented a state collective bargaining law in 1962. Connecticut, Michigan, and Massachusetts passed similar laws in 1965.

In education, collective bargaining followed the right to "meet and confer" with the employer, the only right education employees still have in some states. Meet and confer meant the right of access to petition the employer personally and collectively for improvements in compensation and working conditions. It also meant the right of the employer, the board of education, to ignore these requests in whole or in part. Once collective bargaining entered the scene, teachers were determined to be heard.

After collective bargaining was mandated, teachers saw themselves going from suppliant to partner. However, they felt no confidence that boards of education and administrators would be more willing to share their freedom to determine working conditions than managers and boards in the private sector had been willing to share theirs. Therefore, everything the teachers wanted to change had to go into the contract, or they could not be assured that promises would be kept. In the early days of teacher collective bargaining, every change incorporated into the contract from teacher proposals was viewed by teachers as a victory. Every contract concession made by the board was viewed by them as a loss.

Although the issues in public work were different—there were no profits to be divided up—the mind-sets at the beginning of teacher collective bargaining were not terribly different from the private sector. Teachers felt that school boards, legislators, and community members allowed salaries to be kept low because appropriated state aid was inadequate to support public education properly, and citizens were unwilling to tax themselves locally at a rate sufficient to pay teachers a decent and fair wage. Collective bargaining would be the vehicle to pressure the community and legislators to make adequate funds available to improve the quality of education and also improve the income of teachers. It was helpful that the decade of the 1960s was a time when schools were filled with "baby boom" children. In many communities, more than half of the citizens had children in school, and they were willing to tax both themselves, and those who did not have children in the schools, in order to provide a quality program for their children.

A teacher union representative spoke to a college class in collective bargaining 15 years ago. He was asked by a student unfamiliar with teacher collective bargaining what the union saw as its major obligation in the bargaining process. The union rep, well ahead of his time in seeing the importance of visioning, suggested to the class that they view the collective bargaining process as a marble game. "The board of education has the marbles. It's our job to take them away." The picture (a zero-sum game like marbles) and the process (take-away) were a perfect description of conventional bargaining as then interpreted.

Collective Bargaining Tomorrow: Making the Square Table Round

The century is about to turn. Children growing up at the previous turn of the century knew they would compete for success with the kid next door. Young people in the period prior to World War II expected to compete for jobs with their peers throughout the state. The present generation largely competed with young people throughout the country. Today's children face competition with young people throughout the world. This competition is forcing all institutions to change. Whereas land was the key resource in the 19th century and sophisticated equipment the asset of greatest value in the 20th century, knowledge is becoming the primary capital of the 21st century.

Learning, not schooling, is becoming the focus of societal concern. Although education was formerly seen as a public utility, a function benignly allocated to a governmental monopoly except for the unusual family who chose to pay for the same "utility" twice by sending children to a private school, times are changing rapidly. Even private utility monopolies are no longer what they used to be. AT&T, the monopoly of monopolies, now battles in the marketplace for its share of the economic pie. Telephone, cable, and computer giants battle each other for control of the "information highway."

At the periphery, one can see the "monopoly" of public education beginning to erode. Charter schools, vouchers, privatizing of noneducational functions, and contracting with large private companies such as EAI or subcontracting with Berlitz to deliver elementary foreign language are all relatively recent phenomena. Home schools and private schools in malls, although still a small fraction of the educational delivery system, also suggest that the behemoth of public education is becoming but one option on the education landscape.

School was once defined primarily as a place where young people went to learn. With the advent of modern technology—computer databases, CD-ROMs, the Internet, and other technologies—"school" can be anywhere. The custodial function of schools, offering a safe and secure environment, with food, for children at a time when the two-working-parent family predominates, is important but can be replicated, as the multiplicity of child care enterprises for toddlers demonstrates.

Therefore, the environment in which public education operates is changing. The autonomy of either management or labor to settle a contract or dump the consequences of their disagreement onto students, parents, and the community is now seriously compromised. The national antitax fever, the growing political popularity of financing alternatives to traditional public education, and the general dissatisfaction with the efficacy of public education not only bring into question the viability of teacher strikes, "work-to-rule" actions, or "blackboard flu," they suggest that such actions ultimately can be quite detrimental to the very employees they were designed to help.

Boards of education may conclude erroneously that the changing environment has redressed an imbalance of power. They might conclude that the public, through its elected board, now has rightful control of the public's business. This would be a shortsighted view.

The public's dissatisfaction with its educational system is not targeted at teachers alone. School boards have not escaped public criticism. Several studies, including the Institute for Educational Leadership's *Governing the Public Schools: New Times, New Requirements* (Usdan, Kirst, & Danzberger, 1992) and the *Report of the Twentieth Century Fund Task Force on School Governance* (Twentieth Century Fund, 1992) have called for the abolition of boards of education as we know them, or at least a radical restructuring of boards; for example, creating a board to supervise all human service agencies in the community, including education. States such as Kentucky and Tennessee, which have recently undergone reform of their educational delivery systems, have drastically reduced and refocused the role of boards. These actions are likely harbingers of similar actions to follow in other states.

Have the Purposes of Collective Bargaining Changed?

The basic purposes of bargaining still have relevance for public education because a governmental system, by definition, creates an employer-employee relationship. Bargaining ensures due process rights for employees and gives them a voice in determining compensation and working conditions. Both of these purposes are likely to endure.

One can conceive, and more than a few have advocated, that public school districts should not be primary employers. Rather, it is asserted, boards should hire companies and individuals for fixed-term contracts to provide education in the schools; contracts would be renewed or terminated based on student performance.

Collective bargaining in this scenario would not be public sector bargaining at all but a contract between a private company and its employees—a company that has a fixed-term contract with a board of education to provide services to students. If employees of such companies sought collective bargaining, the bargaining would be conducted under private sector rules.

However, the government employer-employee relationship is likely to persist for a long time to come. It is the nature of that relationship within this rapidly changing social context that can shape the future for school boards, administrators, and unions. The only viable option appears to be a partnership, the same type of relationship that is evolving in the private sector.

Many of the texts describing new directions in private sector bargaining have rediscovered an old idea: worker capitalism, that is, the concept that part of the compensation for all employees would be related to the profitability of the company. Profit sharing would change from a special perquisite of high-level executives to a standard feature of the compensation program of most, if not all, workers. Although still far from a standard practice, the continuous reiteration of this idea in the literature suggests its likely growth as a practice. Its major value is as much symbolic as practical. The idea reinforces in the minds of all the essential partnership of owners, management, and labor in the ultimate success of the enterprise. All win together or lose together.

It is this mind-set of win/win that is at the heart of the necessary new relationship in collective bargaining in public education as well, not because it is trendy but because it is the only viable long-term relationship that will support the present governance structure of public education.

The Need for Partnership

Traditional thinking suggests that the major resource over which conflicts occur in education bargaining is money. Nominally, that is likely true. However, many times, the real issue is power. The distribution of financial resources is only the proximate cause of a more fundamental struggle over who will have the power to shape critical decisions about the district, its employees, and its students.

This power struggle occasionally may be a raw conflict between hostile parties anxious to subdue a disliked antagonist. More likely, teachers feel that their professional competence is ignored in the bureaucratic management structure of the school district. They want their knowledge and competence recognized through contractual assurances of participation in decision making. For boards and their management teams, these positions typically have been viewed as efforts by teachers to make their task easier, not their performance more effective. Too often, both sides see themselves as "keepers of the flame" against a selfish adversary.

Much has been written in recent years about the need to attend to the culture of the school in the process of school improvement. Culture refers to the ways of doing things that are encouraged, or at least sanctioned, by popular opinion. Culture is reflected in behavior and symbols. The symbols that the staff values are an eye into the soul of the school.

The culture and symbols of collective bargaining must change. Only the most cockeyed optimist would expect the resources allocated to public education to grow. The culture of negotiations must therefore move to a concept of partnership. The focus of concern must move from "How much can we get (union) or keep (management/board)?" to "How can we most fairly (to students, staff, and community) and wisely use the resources available to us?" If private industry can adjust to the growing practice of appointing union officials to the governing boards of major corporations, surely boards of education and executive administrators can find similar methods of involving unions not only in matters relating to hours, wages, and working conditions but strategic issues as well. Such a step would not cause a loss of power. It would harness the power of everyone's thinking.

A key issue for future negotiations, such as school improvement, is not power but empowerment, not distrust but a fearless trust in the goodwill of the partner. The challenges that public educators face will require the wisdom of everyone.

However, districts cannot walk to a bargaining Utopia, characterized by full and enduring collaboration. The distance to be traveled toward such a destination is significant, a journey no one has ever completed because it is more a concept than a condition. There are no maps that provide sure guidance to this destination. Many partners who have set forth on this journey have had a difficult pilgrimage. They thought that goodwill and sincere intentions assured them a certain passage from a state of armed truce to full collaboration. Almost always, the partners have been tested together or have tested each other. Often, when a group thought it was making progress, new members joined one or both teams, and ground was lost. The temptation was to abandon the journey; some did. Others looked back at where they had been and realized that it was more dangerous to go back than to go forward. There was no longer a "there" back there. They came to the realization that making the journey, not achieving the destination, brought satisfying and necessary progress.

Summary

When teachers began to push for collective bargaining rights and found an emerging legal climate for this right in a significant number of states, they chose to move in the direction of industrial-style bargaining because industrial bargaining had become the primary form of bargaining in America. In those manufacturing industries subject to union power, salaries and benefits for union employees had become the standard against which all other represented groups compared their own economic progress. Teachers who had completed 4 or more years of college saw that their compensation was significantly lower than that of workers who often had far less formal education. Industrial-style bargaining seemed the method to redress these perceived inequities. However, global competition is fostering some fundamental changes in labor-management relations in the private sector. Significant changes in public sector bargaining are also inevitable as a result of changing social realities. A new partnership of teachers and school boards is necessary, or support for public education can be further eroded.

The next chapters will look at the practical realities of collective bargaining in education in the 21st century.

2

Preparing for Negotiations

The first step in moving toward a cooperative approach to collective bargaining is a decision on the part of both parties that a change in the paradigm is necessary.

Many of the early adopters of a new approach to bargaining did so after a previous contract negotiation that included strikes, court appearances, raucous board meetings, threatened firings, angry demonstrations, and other clear manifestations of a pathological situation. Both parties clearly saw themselves losing in such a scenario. No matter which party got more of its agenda into the final contract, the short-term negatives of anger, anxiety, community dissatisfaction, a critical press, intra-school-board and intraunion conflict, and the long-term certainty of teacher disillusionment and demoralization made any so-called victory at the table a mirage.

In today's environment of national dissatisfaction with public education, the inability to work out accommodations between the parties threatens the very institution of public education. Teachers and board members are becoming more aware of the increasingly tenuous fabric of support they have from the public. They are also realizing that some of the more egregious pathologies seen in school districts with poor labor relations can be seen in less obvious form in their own district. Some of the rot in the relationships is hidden, but it still weakens the foundation of instructional quality and community support for schools. They realize that a ship can sink from an exploding boiler or a small leak in the hull. One pathology just takes longer to work its effects.

Developing a Partnership:
Defining Roles and Learning Skills

Districts interested in a partnership relationship between board and union must decide both alone and together that a new order is necessary. One person can start the process. A union official or board member, a member of the community, or the union's general membership can initiate the dialogue and encourage its development within each body of decision makers. Joint discussions will follow because, like a business partnership, relationships must be carefully thought out and mutual responsibilities defined. If a foundation of goodwill in the previous interactions between the groups does not exist, it is most advisable to hire a consultant to facilitate the development of this new partnership. Considerable knowledge and skill will be necessary to help the parties define their mutual interests in having a new or improved approach to decision making. Sometimes, a staff member, a community member, or a group process specialist from the educational service agency, if one exists in the area, has the background to carry out this role without cost to the district. Perhaps the ideas in this book can provide some useful suggestions if no consultants are available.

Defining Roles

In redesigning the model of collective bargaining into one based on mutual respect, trust, and principled interaction, the concept of partnership must be carefully defined. Who is a partner? Particularly nettlesome questions must be faced anew regarding the roles to be played by the board of education and by the superintendent in the bargaining process.

THE BOARD OF EDUCATION

Much of the literature regarding collective bargaining in education suggests that boards of education should be kept away from the bargaining table. There are several reasons for this view. It is argued that board members often have full-time jobs and therefore lack the time to devote to the process. They also lack the training in bargaining table behavior and techniques; therefore, they can lose their objectivity regarding what is best for the district as a result of heated negotiation sessions. These arguments are substantial. However, if the key parties to the partnership are defined as those who make "final source" decisions, then the board is one of the two essential partners in this relationship. When developing training programs in win/win bargaining, Goldaber and others have insisted that all board members be part of the learning experience because it is the board that makes key decisions and signs the contract. Therefore, it is the board that must make the intellectual commitment to a partnership relationship. In his "communication laboratory" training, Goldaber sat the board and the union leadership in a circle with the superintendent and union executive director at midpoints of the circle across from each other (Wynn, 1983).

It does seem possible to involve the board in the training that builds commitment to cooperative bargaining yet leaves the details of working through the process of reaching agreement on issues to a board team.

THE SUPERINTENDENT

Similarly strong warnings against personal involvement of the superintendent in the negotiation process are widespread. Logical arguments again support this notion if the mode is traditional bargaining. Experts argue that the superintendent is the leader of everyone in the district and should not be identified only as an agent of the board. Involvement of the superintendent in a heated debate with the union bargaining team that leads to a breakoff in talks removes a layer of administration that is available to put the process back on track. Collective bargaining is time consuming and takes the superintendent away from other critical leadership responsibilities for a dangerously long time.

This is all true if the mode of bargaining is traditional and the philosophy is distributional; that is, what "marbles" the teachers get, the board has given up irretrievably. However, if the bargaining table is limited largely to "bread-and-butter" issues and the establishment of problem-solving procedures and processes (see

chapter 5), then the superintendent needs to be involved in dealing
with a resolution of these key strategic issues. Each district will
need to decide how this role will be played, especially if the district
is in transition from a confrontational model of bargaining to a
more integrative process.

PRINCIPALS

Obviously, the board of education, the district's superintendent and his or her immediate staff, and the union's leadership and
bargaining team are key players in bargaining, although roles can
vary widely from place to place. Too often, principals, more and
more recognized in the literature as the catalysts to achieving in-
creased learning, are left out of the bargaining process except, perhaps, for a token principal on the board's bargaining team. Yet they
must deal with the consequences, bad and good, of the negotiated
contract. In rethinking the relationships of bargaining, principals
must be brought into the center of negotiations. Processes that
move problems of teaching and learning away from the bargaining
table and into other problem resolution committees and groups
will enable principals to play their rightful role in advising on key
issues facing the district. To the extent that both parties agree that
site-based decision will be the primary mode of dealing with instructional issues, the opportunity for principals to exert leadership will be enhanced.

Learning to Work Together

Fisher and Ury (1981) widely promulgated the notion that a
different style of bargaining had to focus less on positions the sides
took at the table and more on the basic interests of the parties that
gave rise to these positions. They wisely argued that parties cannot
agree on a proper solution until they have a similar understanding
of a problem as the other side views it.

An effective way to create this mind-set would be to bring representatives of both parties to an off-site facility for a weekend
seminar that would be designed primarily for the parties, alone

and together, to engage in a series of role-playing or brainstorming activities and joint discussions. Sometimes, such training is available from the state labor relations board. A number of private contractors have built an expertise in this area, and a few districts have called on the Harvard Negotiations Project staff to do this training. A long weekend learning to work together can be the ideal setting for a new beginning.

Basic Training

One of the first goals of such training is the development of mutually agreed-upon objectives for collaboration. A facilitator can work the groups through a process that reviews or develops the district vision. A review of the district's strengths, weaknesses, opportunities, and threats builds a common perception of the environment in which education must operate. All of these activities become preliminary to building a set of common objectives for cooperative bargaining. Such objectives might include the following:

- To use the talents of employees most effectively
- To improve the quality of instruction available to students
- To enhance the sense of employment security for staff
- To increase personal satisfaction in being a member of the teaching profession
- To use limited resources wisely (Woodworth & Meek, 1995, p. 35)

These objectives become the touchstone against which each party can judge the quality and effectiveness of the ongoing relationship. When the parties face difficult times, they can frame their problems within the background of their mutual agreement on essential purposes. Going back to first principles does help.

People do not intuitively know how to work well together, especially in a business relationship. Therefore, the parties will want to assess their skills in communication, listening, and problem solving. Few persons elected to boards of education should be expected to have had any formal training in these easy-to-identify but difficult-to-execute skills. Most educators have not had exposure to formalized instruction in these areas. It is impossible for an individual to move to a new set of behaviors if he or she has never learned constructive skills nor had the opportunity to practice them in a "safe" environment. Both parties need to recognize the truth of Peter Senge's (1990, p. 198) aphorism that "advocacy without inquiry begets more advocacy," a negative behavior pattern so universal that he describes it as a systems problem that underlies much of the conflict within and between many organizations.

Several current problems that might normally appear in negotiations can be used as case studies. For example, participants can be asked to sit in a circle with board members or administrators and teacher bargainers in alternate chairs. The facilitator asks a teacher to identify a district problem and suggest a solution. The next person in line (a board member or administrator) must either agree to the proposed solution or present an alternative solution. The process continues around the group until a solution is agreed on by all sitting at the table. The facilitator records all proposed solutions. If no consensus solution emerges, the group has a list of options for further study should the problem actually appear in negotiations.

Targeted Training

Another exercise in problem solving would have the board or administration team and the union team meet separately, possibly each with a facilitator. Each group would be asked to imagine it was the other party preparing for the next round of negotiations. The board team, for example, would role-play the union team and attempt to identify the significant *needs and interests* that the union might be likely to identify. The board or administrator group would then discuss *why* the union team is likely to identify each need or interest in order to try to understand its thinking. The team would then identify its own needs and interests in the next round of bargaining. Areas of congruence with the projected union list might lead to a discussion of strategies to facilitate quick agreement in these areas of shared concern. Discussion within the board or administrative team would then address those areas that might be unacknowledged by the union. Here again, strategies for responding to the items on this list are brainstormed. The same process takes place within the union team's meeting. The groups would then meet together and compare and contrast their perceptions of their own needs and interests and those of the other party.

As a final step of what is a training exercise, not a negotiating session, balanced groups of union members and the board and its team would be organized to discuss together possible ways of responding to a few of these nonmutual needs and interests identified in the first exercise. Groups would be challenged to identify how an *objective measure or measures* could be found to judge the likely effectiveness of a proposed strategy in responding to an identified need. For example, if the union identified common planning time at the elementary level as a need of teachers, an objective standard for a solution might be the experience of a neighboring district in rearranging the hours of the school day, descriptions in the professional literature about the effectiveness of different approaches to scheduling teachers, or the advice of a professor from a local university known for his or her expertise in the area of elementary education.

Other Training Options

There is another form of training that can be useful in helping to establish the necessary mind-set for successful cooperative bargaining. It could be used in conjunction with the above-described efforts to create mutually shared objectives for engaging in win/win bargaining and to help both parties see the world from the other side's perspective. The technique is generically called *game playing*. Game theory crosses a number of disciplines including mathematics, psychology, and other fields. Much work in this field has been done with the assistance of computers (Allman, 1984).

Two games in particular have become well-known training tools. They are especially useful for training in cooperative bargaining because they are "mixed-motive" rather than "zero-sum" games. In the zero-sum games, one plays to win. If the player does not win, he or she loses. In mixed-motive games, the player's fate is somewhat determined by how the other individual or group assesses its own options. One popular game or simulation is called "The Prisoner's Dilemma," another "Win As Much As You Can."

In the original "Prisoner's Dilemma" game, two suspects of a crime are captured and separated. There is not enough evidence to convict them at trial, although there is a certainty on the part of the authorities that they are both guilty. Each is told separately that if both confess, they will be prosecuted, but authorities will recommend a reduced sentence (e.g., 5 years of imprisonment). If neither confesses, then each will be prosecuted on a lesser charge and receive less jail time (2 years of imprisonment each). However, if one confesses and the other does not, then the confessor will receive very lenient treatment (1 year of imprisonment) and the other will get much harsher punishment (10 years of imprisonment). The best joint outcome is for both not to confess. The best individual outcome is for one to confess and the other not to confess. Individuals are asked to decide what they will do, and the parties are then brought together to discuss their options.

Choosing a behavior in this game requires an analysis of the thinking, motives, and trustworthiness of the other party. Research has shown that the behavior of both parties can be shaped by the instructions given them; for example, if each is told that he or she should try to get a shorter sentence than the opponent, both almost always confess. The result is a 5-year sentence for both, much worse than if both had agreed not to confess. In other words, both can achieve a reasonably favorable outcome only by agreeing to cooperate. However, that outcome will not happen if each is suspicious of the trustworthiness of the other. The game can be revised for use as a training exercise because there are many variations of the game that can be played for points (Allman, 1984).

Another mixed-motive game is "Win As Much As You Can." In this game, groups are formed, given a red and green card, and told that each group is to win as many points as it can. Each group must decide whether to show a red or green card when requested to do so by the facilitator. Points to be awarded can be determined based on the number of groups in the simulation. For example, if three groups are playing and all groups show a red card, all groups might lose 10 points. If all groups show green cards, all win 10 points. If one group shows a red card and the other two groups show a green card, the team with the red card wins 30 points and the teams showing the green cards lose 10 points. If two groups show a red card and one shows a green card, the teams with the red cards win 10 points and the green group loses 30 points.

Extensive research has been done on both games. Computer programs have been written by experts from a variety of disciplines to find the best way to "win." Research has shown that the best way to achieve the goal of the game, "Win As Much As You Can," is to seek to cooperate with the other party on the first iteration and then do what the other party does in subsequent moves. If both parties decide to cooperate from the first iteration, they maximize their score. Because computers are never jealous of what the other computer is scoring, the computer can be programmed to stick to its game plan. There is an obvious lesson here for human beings.

The single best way for each group to win as much as it can is to show green the first time, hope the other parties also show green, and keep showing green for the duration of the activity.

Several important insights can be generated out of such training experiences. Parties can learn that it is in their long-term best interest to cooperate rather than compete. They also can learn together that encouraging a continuing positive response from the other side fosters its own long-term self-interest. Learning that both sides are advantaged by cooperating helps eliminate the natural good guy (us)/bad guy (them) mentality that can negatively affect everything that goes on in a negotiating relationship (Kohn, 1986).

Research has also shown that people who see their long-term success based on an enduring relationship are more likely to be committed to the relationship. Cohabiting couples split up much more than married couples. One contract negotiated in a spirit in which each party takes seriously and responds positively to the needs of the other is likely to produce more contracts negotiated in this manner. The parties slowly become confident that cooperation is the best way for both to "win."

Summary

Creating a relationship based on cooperation where little or none has existed before is a difficult, somewhat risky, and always time-consuming process. Although training can improve old skills and add new ones, the fundamental relationship, a partnership based on enlightened self-interest, like a marriage, cannot be built on a written document. Negotiators on both sides of the table need to internalize the perilous environment of public support in which they operate and build a mind-set that recognizes that whether in games or in life, more gets done through cooperation than conflict. In public education, there appears to be no other viable long-term choice.

Bargaining table behavior, the next topic, is the key to enhancing or destroying good intentions.

3

The Bargaining Process: Less Is More

The Chicago School District endured nine strikes in 18 years. Each time the school district went on strike, the mayor's office intervened and "found" money that settled the strike. After this scenario happened once or twice, the union learned how to play the game. This situation seems to suggest that confrontation is effective; in the long run, it is not.

With a substantial number of parents and business leaders convinced that the schools were not achieving their purposes, compounded by Secretary of Education William Bennett's pronouncement that Chicago had "the worst schools in America" (Hess, 1991, p. 6), governance of public education soon was effectively removed from the board of education. Each school was to be run by a council controlled by parents and community members. Teachers were to be a minority on such councils. Principals lost their tenure guarantees. They were to be employed for a fixed period of time by the community council. By mid-1995, the 15-member board of education had been dissolved, replaced by a panel of five members named by the mayor. A new law limited issues that can be placed on the bargaining table by the union and prohibited strikes for 18 months.

Confrontation had worked for a while, but in the long run, the public rebelled. It is not yet clear whether public education will be better or worse under this new governance system. Clearly, the school board lost credibility and power, and then its very existence. For better or worse, principals lost job protection guarantees. Teachers have less position security than before. This case study may be a harbinger of what confrontational bargaining, especially when coupled with public dissatisfaction, may produce in the future.

If political wisdom seems to call for more cooperation at the bargaining table, how can it be done?

Starting With Beliefs and First Principles

Probably the healthiest first step that a union and board or management team can take when initiating formal bargaining, if this activity was not part of a training program prior to entering negotiations, is to identify and discuss the basic beliefs and concepts that undergird the need to make bargaining a cooperative process and the difficulties that will be faced by both sides as the process proceeds. Identified below are a few such issues that need to be faced.

School Reform Is No Longer a Bargainable Issue

Since the publication of *A Nation at Risk* in 1983 by the United States Commission on Excellence in Education, state after state has engaged in "restructuring" and "reform" efforts to such a profound degree that state legislatures have, in many instances, become de facto state boards of education. Governors have become functional state superintendents of public instruction. Public education reform initiatives have defined educational policy requirements to such an extent that local officials, board members, and union representatives have relatively little flexibility to determine many key issues, such as length of the academic year and curriculum requirements, which are now often mandated by the state. State proficiency tests have become almost more important than local school district requirements in determining graduation eligibility. It is in the interest of both parties to work to ensure student success by using the narrow scope of issues still left for local determination to their mutual benefit. Unions are responding to these changed circumstances. Albert Shanker, president of the American Federation of Teachers (AFT), moved his organization to a proactive position on the school reform debate several years ago. The National Education Association (NEA), the nation's largest teachers union, announced a staff reorganization to foster improved school quality only recently, at their annual convention in the summer of 1995.

Both Sides Will Lose Some Control
Within an Empowered School District

There are school board members and school administrators who feel that some of the current major restructuring initiatives, such as site-based decision making and teacher empowerment, are Trojan horses under which guise the union can gain power over the school district that it could not get at the bargaining table. This view badly misunderstands the reality of these concepts. In most districts where site-based decision making has really taken hold, teachers have the right to petition *either* the administration or board to waive a policy *or* the union to waive a contract provision if necessary to implement a teacher-driven decision about the school program. The credibility of both is at stake in responding to these requests.

Cooperative Bargaining Presents Problems
for Both Parties

A naive view of collective bargaining sees this process as essentially bipolar: board versus teachers, union versus management. This view is inaccurate. As the Chicago scenario suggests, the public may tolerate being left out of the process when things are working smoothly. When trouble results, they will be heard. So-called sunshine laws in Florida and other locations, which require that collective bargaining be carried out in public, are on the books because the public interest can be ignored only so long.

An examination of the internal dynamics of each of the main parties to negotiations shows that bipolarity is a simplification and a misconception. Management often must represent a board that has its own bipolarity, split among "hardliners" and "conciliators." The management team can have rifts among those from central office, who take a more conceptual view of issues because they do not have to deal with the day-to-day consequences of implementing a proposed policy, and building leaders, who do. Teacher unions face the same problem. It is not uncommon to find teacher negotiating teams made up of one or more of the district's well-known malcontents who use the negotiating experience as an opportunity to settle scores or stall change. Union leadership is often incapable of preventing election or selection of such people to a bargaining team.

Both parties must be sure they have prepared their constituents for a new approach to bargaining before getting started, and they must continue the education process as the negotiations continue. A questionnaire to union members that seeks to confirm a general support for a less confrontational model of bargaining might be a good starting point to assure everyone that leaders are not too far ahead of their followers. If support for such an approach is not evident, then the union has its own education problem even before starting talks with the board.

Both Parties Need to Be Cautious About Trumpeting News of a "New Relationship"

The Rochester, New York, collective bargaining agreement was signed in 1987 with a flourish of publicity about a new age of joint responsibility for educational improvement among teachers, administrators, and board members. Among its many innovative provisions were a career ladder for teachers, school-based planning, and many other initiatives unusual or unique in the late 1980s. (It also included a 40% increase in salary for teachers over the 3 years of the contract.) Not long after this tidal wave of publicity, parents and community began to ask "Where's the beef?" With all of this goodwill, everyone expected big results. When they were not immediately forthcoming, at least some members of the community felt they had been misled (Kerchner & Koppich, 1993).

When initiating a cooperative bargaining relationship, both parties can be best served by focusing on the real reasons they are pursuing an integrative approach to bargaining and constantly striving to ensure that everyone understands these reasons. The results might best be left to speak for themselves. Premature rejoicing about a "new era" may be the prelude to a big fall.

The Future Will Look a Lot Less Like the Present Than the Present Looks Like the Past

Collective bargaining is a process with a 60-year history. Law, rules, procedures, and agencies all have been built on experiences from this past. Whatever its faults, everyone knows what to expect from the old system. A large cadre of people makes its living from understanding how to use the old system. A new system, on the other hand, is a risk for everyone. There are no models of unqualified success to guide those heading down this path. Only by agreeing together that technology or privatization or charter schools or other factors, singly or together, are going to have a profound effect on the delivery of education can everyone be assured that the risks are worth the effort.

Managing Meetings

Much has been made in this chapter about fundamental issues such as beliefs about collective bargaining within the current climate for public education and the shifting sources of power within the larger political environment. This focus is necessary because no portfolio of cooperative bargaining techniques will suffice if both parties do not have an intellectual confidence in what they are doing. However, techniques do matter. A well-run meeting is likely to accomplish its goals. A poorly run meeting can start a relationship on the way to disaster. Some essential issues need to be decided before the process starts. Some of these ideas are not dissimilar to processes often used in traditional bargaining.

The Teams

The two parties should agree on the composition and size of the teams before negotiations start. Both sides should also agree as to when outside resource people will be permitted to join the meetings. The invitation to nonteam members should be issued by consensus. The role of individuals of "special significance" in bargaining sessions—school board members, the superintendent, the union president—should be clarified at the outset if a decision is made not to include them as part of the regular bargaining teams.

The Meetings

Meetings should not be happenings but planned events. Coleadership of the sessions fosters the partnership goal of the total process. For clarity, it might be useful to alternate the role of chair rather than to try to have two people run one meeting. The group might decide that, rather than select two permanent cochairs, each side will rotate among its members the responsibility for conducting a meeting when its turn comes.

Positive feelings among the parties will be enhanced if a meeting schedule is adopted and a time frame for each meeting is rigidly enforced. Changes in the length of meetings should be made only by consensus agreement of both parties. Rigid limits on the amount of time a meeting may be extended, if adopted at the beginning of the process, keep everyone focused on arriving at solutions, not talking.

The Meeting Agenda

The agenda for the next meeting should be decided by consensus. One good way to manage issues is to ask each party, at the first meeting, to bring to the table all the problems it wishes to resolve. The problems should be classified as "major issues," "important issues," and "minor issues." By working through minor issues alternately brought to the table by each team at the beginning of the process, a momentum of success can be built for dealing with the "major issues."

Decision Making

Each problem is resolved through a consensus process. Consensus is defined as a solution that is sufficiently acceptable to *everyone* at the table, and all can agree to support it. If a consensus decision is not possible, the matter is held over to another meeting or referred to a jointly appointed and balanced study committee reporting to the two teams. Brainstorming and other group process techniques will be the preferred study mode. The parties will always seek objective criteria by which to evaluate proposed solutions.

Caucusing

Caucusing by parties during the negotiation process is a quintessential feature of traditional bargaining. Secrecy, scheming, and surprising are all artifacts of the process of caucusing. Does caucusing have any place in a true partnership in which both parties are committed to helping each other resolve problems? Probably not at the theoretical level. But teacher union bargainers and administrators do not live only at a theoretical level. They must balance theory with the contingencies of real situations. Teacher bargainers at the table may feel comfortable that both parties have successfully arrived at a solution to a problem brought to the table by the administration. But they are not individually at ease that a solution should be accepted until they talk to their colleagues on the team privately and question whether more educational work needs to be done with the membership before a decision is made. This is but one example of a situation when a caucus might make sense.

The best approach may be to discuss together the possible negative effects that frequent caucusing can bring and then agree to allow it by consensus agreement of both parties.

Confidentiality

This can be a difficult issue. People need the freedom to question hard and object forcefully in the early stages of discussion as part of the normal process of seeking a good decision. But context

is everything. The statement of one individual of either party
quoted to a larger audience without an explanation of the full evolution of the discussion can be misleading and possibly fatal to
broad support for the work of the teams. On the other hand, undue
secrecy can create suspicion in the minds of those not at the table.
Those who were negative to a nonconfrontational style of bargaining at the beginning can exploit such situations to undermine what
is actually a productive process for both parties.

One approach to the issue of confidentiality is to agree to a set
of minutes that describes the issues that are being discussed by the
parties. Teams can decide whether minutes should include actual
table agreements or just general information that an issue has been
resolved. No specific comments, positions, or arguments would be
recorded.

Working Together

Effective meeting management must operate concurrently
with shared understandings about expectations as the process
moves along. Some general principles can help guide the interre-
lationships of the parties during the negotiation process.

1. Facilitate the Growth of Trust; Don't Demand It

Trust is earned, not given. People cannot truly agree to trust
each other. Trust is both an intellectual and emotional response.
Trust, like love, grows over time. Nevertheless, individuals can act
in a loving manner even before genuine love develops. Negotiating teams can promise to respond to events in a trusting manner,
even if they have not yet developed an intellectual conviction that
trust is warranted. They can promise to act in such a way as to earn
the other party's trust. But sincere trust can only be the product of
an enduring relationship in which people respond out of trust and
act in a trust-generating manner. Trust will grow if both parties
work from the minimal assumption that the other party has at least
a selfish interest in making a cooperative negotiation work.

2. Separate Resource-Allocation Issues From Problem-Resolution Issues

The best place to begin a new approach to collective bargaining would be with problems that are not resource based. It is hoped that many such problems would end up classified as either "minor issues" or "important issues," but not "major issues," as suggested earlier.

It is possible to argue that all problems can be defined as resource based in that almost all problems can be solved if the district has enough money. Nevertheless, issues related to contract interpretation (whether or not teachers have to report to school when a snow day has been declared for students), policy implementation (the extent to which English teachers can select supplementary books for their students to read without board approval under the district's textbook adoption policy), and administrative consistency (teachers in some schools have received a written reprimand for chronic lateness, whereas latecomers in other schools have gone largely unnoticed) are not essentially issues involving the allocation of resources. If necessary, a study committee that draws on the experience and perceptions of those not at the table can be established to look at an issue. Committee recommendations for dealing with the problem studied can be offered to the bargainers.

The ultimate goal ought to be removing such issues from the collective bargaining process completely by creating sustained problem resolution processes and structures that can operate in good faith outside of master contract requirements. It has long been said that the depth of the trust between teachers and management is in inverse relationship to the size of the contract. The statement is most certainly true.

3. Start by Exchanging Problems, Not Solutions

Fisher and Ury (1981) urge that negotiators seek first to understand the "interests" of the other parties rather than responding to their "positions" at the table. It is best for both parties to start with a definition of their interests without stating them in bargaining-position form. Interests can be thought of as needs that are unmet or as problems that are unresolved. By putting problems before the group, an issue that starts out as one party's problem can become owned by both parties. One effective way to present problems at the bargaining table is to express an issue in the following manner:

1. This is our problem.
2. These are the reasons that this issue is a problem for us.
3. Here are the facts that demonstrate that this is a problem.

The other party is likely to respond in an objective manner to a problem presented with specific case facts. (Patterson, 1993).

4. Brainstorm Solutions for Problems

Nothing symbolizes more clearly the adversarial nature of collective bargaining than the reality of the bargaining table. The management team sits on one side, the union team on the other: Us and Them. A significant departure in this mind-set can be achieved by simply changing the placement of team members at the table. Requiring that bargainers from each team take every other seat will go a long way toward creating a climate of cohesiveness rather than opposition.

One first step to dealing with problems is to go around the table allowing each person to identify one, and only one, problem. As stated elsewhere, this might best be something less than a major problem. All problems are recorded on a flip chart. No distinction is made as to whether administrators or union members identified a problem. After the problem-identification process is completed, one member at the table is asked to identify a problem from the flip chart and offer a solution. A person next to the first individual must critique the proposed solution. If this person agrees with the solution, the next person in line speaks. If the proposed solution is agreed on around the table, the issue is resolved. If one of the speakers objects to the proposed solution, this person is required to offer an alternative solution. If the person next to this individual does not like the newly proffered solution, then this person must offer a different suggestion to the group. The process continues around the table until a mutually agreeable solution is developed. If no solution is possible, then a more broadly based study committee can be organized with a report made back to both teams.

5. *Freely Share Relevant Information*

It has been traditional to share with the other party at the table only that information that cannot be withheld or that furthers the interests of the party holding the information. Some information is "spoon-fed" to the other party, bits and pieces being released only when it is self-serving to do so.

Cooperation and trust are impossible if the parties believe that the other side is hiding information or distorting it, even if not technically lying. It is not unlikely that traditional attitudes toward collective bargaining will be most difficult to modify relative to information sharing, especially budget information. If the parties cannot agree to share all information in the early stages of a new relationship, it is important that both parties be candid about what will and will not be shared. At least this information can be trusted. No sustainable mutual effort to solve problems together can be expected until both parties feel confidence in sharing all necessary and available information with the other party.

Getting to a Contract

What, then, should be done with issues that remain unresolved, especially resource allocation issues? The best approach is to use a technique often used in expedited bargaining. Both sides agree to set a time limit for reaching an agreement, such as 3 weeks. If all remaining issues are not "major" ones, the sides can agree to limit the number of issues that each may bring to the table. Then the processes used before are repeated in a somewhat more formalized manner:

1. Each side explains a problem (the need for a salary increase) and the reason it considers the matter a problem (the cost of

living has gone up 3% in the last year), and then provides information that might show why the matter is a problem (reports from the federal government on the Consumer Price Index; settlements from neighboring districts recognizing the issue of cost of living).

2. The other party shares any problems that are similar. (The cost of living has gone up, affecting everything the district buys, but state aid has gone down.)

3. The parties attempt to assess the meaning of the issue in terms of its *strategic* impact on the district. (Teachers' view: If the district does not maintain salary parity with other districts, talented people will leave and the "best and the brightest" of the new crop of teachers will not come to the district. Board view: If the district has to cut programs, such as athletics, and services, such as bus transportation, to pay a salary increase it cannot afford this year, the district may generate lasting enmity from the taxpayers, which could hurt pending bond issues to build new schools and purchase technology.)

4. Both try to find a solution that responds to their jointly developed goals statement and the political exigencies of dealing with their constituencies. The fairness of proposed solutions to these problems is always tested, insofar as possible, by some objective standard or process to which both parties can agree. A fair *standard* for the appropriateness of a salary increase might be the average increase given in the area to teachers in districts that have *the same or very similar economic characteristics*. A fair *process* might be jointly agreeing to use a retired educator as an informal fact finder on the dispute. (See chapter 4 for further elaboration of this suggestion.)

Summary

Leaders of teacher unions and school boards and their management need to redesign their relationship and find new ways to solve problems and ensure the rights of all. Joint training in new ideas and new approaches to problem solving can help significantly in creating a positive climate for bargaining. Some of the older traditions of collective bargaining will endure, at least for a while. A sustained growth in trust between the parties and a joint effort to achieve solutions that recognize the needs of both parties can make even old techniques look new.

The next chapter will consider strategies for dealing with those issues that simply cannot be resolved by the parties without outside assistance.

4

Managing Conflict

The basic premise of bargaining in a win/win mode is the assumption that both parties see the best interests of their constituents most efficiently served by helping the other party meet the interests of its own constituents simultaneously. Previous chapters have shown that this assumption has been proven intellectually sound. The parties join together to attempt to achieve the joint resolution of problems, including the fair and proper distribution of the district's resources, because, at least in the long run, it is in the separate interest of each party to do so.

The assertion of a joint belief in the superiority of bargaining *with* rather than bargaining *against* the other party in no way suggests a companion belief that both parties are thereby guaranteed a positive result for their efforts. Conflict is a normal characteristic of human interaction. Occasional conflict is not, per se, a culpable fault of either party. The lack of knowledge about how to manage conflict in constructive ways and for constructive ends *is* a censurable weakness. The purpose of this chapter is to suggest win/win methods for dealing with conflict whether it arises when trying to agree to a master contract or whether it surfaces when living with the contract.

The focus here will not be on conventional approaches to conflict resolution as used in traditional bargaining—mediation, fact finding, and arbitration—as they are usually practiced. A library full of books and journal articles has been written about these processes. This section will look at approaches to these topics that are more in keeping with an effort on the part of both parties to find a way to reach a mutually satisfactory solution yet take advantage of well-worn paths where some of the brambles have been removed by a long history of use.

Resolving Conflicts: A General Perspective

Chapter 2 noted the importance of training both parties in communication skills and problem-solving techniques as part of the process of creating a cooperative relationship in bargaining. Communication skills are important because language is a window to the mind. It is possible to view the other's thinking only through the verbal expression of that thinking or the behavior of that individual. Collective bargaining is, by its very nature, essentially a verbal activity. Listening carefully is a critical aspect of using language to interpret thinking, so it is important to problem resolution. But listening alone will not ensure understanding.

Reflecting on what is heard and processing the messages are important as well. When a search for common interests proves fruitless, further analysis of the conflict is imperative. Only through genuine understanding of the thinking of the other side can empathy be developed and other solution possibilities generated. The best way to achieve that understanding is to imagine oneself facing an issue as the other side views it and feels it. For example, a seemingly irresolvable problem might present itself as follows:

- THE BOARD'S POSITION: Because of the unique nature of magnet schools, the board should have an unimpeded right to select teachers for the new magnet school it is creating in the fall.
- THE UNION'S POSITION: The seniority of teachers with appropriate certification shall be the controlling force in selecting staff for a new magnet school.

In another of the many publications from Harvard University regarding negotiations, Fisher, Kopelman, and Schneider (1994)

suggest using what they call the Currently Perceived Choice (CPC)
format as a method of trying to understand on a deep level the
position of the other side in international disputes. Their "Consequences . . . But . . ." format is presented here as a tool to seek further understanding of the other side's position in situations in
which the normal brainstorming or search for objective criteria to
resolve problems has not moved the parties to agreement, or at
least not yet. It represents yet another technique to encourage each
side to not only understand but empathize with the problem as the
other side must deal with it. The protocol for a school board team
to analyze the magnet school staffing problem is as follows:

The Union View	Our View
Perceptions:	Perceptions:
Values:	Values:
Feelings:	Feelings:
Consequences if the union says YES to the board's position (list):	Consequences if the board says NO to the union's position (list):
BUT:	BUT:

The board team would then imagine that it is, in fact, the union
team and attempt to analyze the proposal from their view. For example, it would list the negative consequences to the union if the
board's position were to be accepted as proposed. It would then
list the positives for the union of acquiescing, even if a small list,
under the BUT section. Then, analyzing the issue from its own
point of view, the board team would list under the "Consequences" column the consequences of continuing to oppose the
union's position and list the positive aspects of acquiescing to the
union's view under the BUT category. The board team's analysis of
the union's thinking might look as follows:

- *Perception:* If they (the union) do not support seniority in this
  instance, they will be violating a sacred principle of unionism.

- *Values:* Seniority is one of the fundamental principles for which unions have long stood.
- *Feelings:* Many teachers, especially more senior staff, will feel the union has betrayed them.

It is relatively easy for a board to understand why a union would support seniority assignment in this case. It is a quite richer perception to understand the value system that drives the union's position and the dangers the union feels it might face if it accedes to the board's view. This type of analysis can lead to more brainstorming of options by both parties.

Conflicts Over Interests

Avoiding Win/Lose Choices

Fisher and Ury (1981) identified the acronym BATNA—the best alternative to a negotiated agreement—as an important tool in the arsenal of bargainers who, no matter how sincere their efforts to reach a contract that responds to the fundamental interests of both parties, are unsuccessful. This unhappy result may occur either because the parties ran out of time or ideas in the effort to find mutually acceptable solutions or, despite the best efforts of one side, the other party could not be convinced to give the win/win approach a chance. Ultimately, one of the parties may be forced to make a difficult but straightforward choice; for example, the board team may have to choose whether to take a strike or give in to the other side's demands.

Frustration is a likely result of unsuccessful efforts to move the discussion away from an adversarial climate. It is too easy to succumb to feelings and emotions rather than to continue to use rational strategies to find agreement. Management trainees are sometimes exposed to the "dollar game" to prove this point. (Because of inflation, the point might better be made in a "20-dollar game"!)

In the dollar game, a group is invited to bid on a dollar that will be made available at auction. A requirement of the game is that the *second* lowest bidder pay to the auctioneer his or her last bid as the auctioneer's fee. The winner pays no fee. The opportunity to get a dollar for a nickel or dime or a quarter at the beginning of the auction is very attractive. However, as the game progresses, bidders realize that they must continue to bid, no longer to get the dollar (to win) but to avoid the cost of paying the auctioneer's fee with nothing to show for it (to lose). The mental set moves away from trying to win the game toward strategy that seeks to avoid losing (Susskind & Cruikshank, 1987).

The point of this anecdote is simple. Although a party committed to cooperative bargaining may feel frustration in not getting the other side to play win/win, the team must be careful lest it get drawn inadvertently into willing participation in a win/lose scenario.

However, even if both parties are making a totally conscientious effort to find mutually satisfying solutions to issues, the search may be unsuccessful, at least in part. There are some approaches to dispute resolution that can be useful.

Settling Conflicts Through Win/Win Choices

Three options are available to negotiating parties who have been unable to resolve their disputes.

1. Keep using or adapting long-recognized group process methods to solve problems, or invent new methods to keep the parties focused on finding ways to accommodate the *interests* (needs) of both parties.
2. Reconcile the issue based on a determination of which side is *right*. Courts, state labor relations officials, and independent arbitrators are available to make findings. If a determination of winners and losers is necessary, these bodies can adjudicate unfair labor practice charges, interpret laws and administrative rulings, or render decisions that have the force of law. This last category includes arbitration awards.
3. Reconcile the issue based on *power*. Power may be as benign a technique as putting an issue to a vote (of the union, of the citizens) or as brutal a procedure as a protracted strike or a "work-to rule" job action intended to force the board of edu-

cation to accept a contract (Cohen-Rosenthal & Burton, 1987).

The goal of cooperative bargaining is to keep the dispute in the first category or, at worst, the second, pursuing a search for solutions that respond to the needs of both parties and that can be achieved together. It is possible to use some of the conventional techniques of dispute resolution in unconventional ways to achieve that goal.

Mediation

Normally, mediation is provided under the auspices of the state labor relations department or commission. These agencies often can provide skilled and experienced individuals who provide needed assistance to achieve an agreement. But prior agreements to "solve it ourselves" can permit more innovative approaches.

For example, the consultant who did training for the parties in collaborative decision making and/or problem solving prior to the start of negotiations, if such training occurred, could, by prior agreement, be invited into a seeming impasse situation to act as a mediator and facilitate the search for solutions in those areas that have proven most intractable. Another option is to choose as mediator or facilitator a community member who is experienced in staff training and problem solving in the private sector. The parties might invite a retired administrator and teacher to work as a team to facilitate dispute resolution.

Joint Fact Finding

Traditional fact finding is also provided, usually through a state agency. Both parties are often reluctant to move to traditional fact finding for several reasons. It can be seen as a sign of failure, either to the parties themselves or perhaps to the community, which, in all likelihood, will not be thrilled about bringing in someone from outside the community to tell elected officials and appointed staff how to solve a local problem or spend district dollars.

There is an element of risk because the values and biases of the fact finder may be unknown or, if known, antithetical to the interests of one of the parties. Here again, prior to embarking on the negotiation process, both parties can agree to a joint fact-finding process that actually might be included in the mediation stage. The activity would be designed to answer the following questions:

- What do we already know about the problem, and on what basis do we conclude that we have valid and reliable information?
- What do we not know about the issue? Where can we find the information we need?

The facilitator could be authorized to employ a third party or agency, such as a university, to conduct any research that might be relevant to the problem.

A more formal approach to fact finding could be built on choosing a prominent and well-respected local individual or individuals to serve as fact finder(s). This keeps the process under the control of the parties and maintains the local connection in the decision-making process.

Some local courts have found an analogous approach increasingly attractive as a method to reduce dockets. Before a case can come to trial, it must go to mediation. This is actually a process that combines mediation and fact finding.

If the economic issues are relatively small, or the case is not too technically challenging, an attorney selected by the court attempts to help the parties resolve their dispute. (In more significant cases, three attorneys, one nominated by each party and a third, selected by the other two attorneys, are used.) The mediator or mediating team reads briefs presented by each side and then questions both parties further. By pointing out weaknesses in both cases, the mediator attempts to bring the parties to a settlement on their own. If no agreement is possible, an "award" is made, an offer of settlement that the mediator believes will be the likely result if the case goes to trial. There are severe financial penalties imposed on either side if it does not accept the award and then is unsuccessful in getting a significantly better settlement when a trial is concluded. In one jurisdiction, a monetary award in court that is less than 10% above the mediator's suggested settlement requires the complainant to pay the legal fees that the defendant incurred during the court procedure.

In a school application, the mediator/fact finders could be jointly selected by the parties and could function in similar fashion by challenging the assumptions and data of each party.

Arbitration

Arbitration of school district labor disputes is normally performed either by a state government official assigned to this task or by the American Arbitration Association (AAA). The former process involves some degree of chance as to who will be assigned; the latter process can be very expensive. Both approaches, in a sense, speak to a failure of the parties to resolve their own dispute. Nevertheless, in dire circumstances, a safety net is necessary.

Here again, formal, standardized processes can be reinvented for the purposes of the local parties. For example, both parties could agree that the final "award" of the fact finder would become the mutually accepted final resolution of issues for which no mutually agreeable solutions could be found by the parties. In effect, fact finding, through mutual agreement, takes on the functions of binding arbitration. In this process, the binding decision is made by local parties known to and respected by both sides. If they so chose, both sides could agree that the fact finder(s) would be limited to choosing between either party's position on each issue in the fact-finding process—in effect, creating a "last best offer" option. It is interesting to note that State of Iowa arbitrators working in a last best offer mode may choose any one of *three* options: the employer's position, the employee's position, or the fact finder's position. If the parties were to agree voluntarily to such a third option even for conventional arbitration, they might help overcome some of the criticisms of last best offer arbitration as it operates in most environments today. (In last best offer arbitration, the deciding party may choose only the last offer of either party. A compromise solution, or what Goldaber called a "newpromise," a creative solution to a dispute, may not be proposed by the arbitrator.)

Conflicts Over Existing Contracts

Prevention

The best approach to dealing with conflicts over already existing contracts is *prevention*. The first step in a prevention strategy is to ensure that everyone knows the meaning and intent of each article in the contract.

The teacher union can make its contribution to this joint goal by reviewing the total contract with all teachers, a common practice once an agreement has been signed, and following up this activity with an in-depth review with building representatives, the first individuals who will be queried if a teacher feels that he or she has been aggrieved.

The burden of explaining the contract is even greater on the administration. Trouble is most likely to start through some inadvertent action of a principal. Too often, the principal is acting out of ignorance rather than a deliberate intention to violate the contract. If "location, location, location" are the three most important factors in having a successful restaurant, "intention, intention, intention" are the three most important words in understanding the contract. Everyone needs to know what the parties had in mind when they accepted the language of each article. If midlevel administrators have been properly involved when working with the union toward a mutually satisfactory contract, contract misinterpretation becomes less of a problem than if principals have been largely ignored.

Training

It is not uncommon to find that unions do a better job of training staff in contract implementation than do school leaders in training supervisory staff. The result is a needless escalation of small problems into large ones. If the principal or other supervisor understands the contract fully and is schooled in techniques for making a grievance hearing a search for a mutually satisfactory resolution of identified difficulties, most problems can be resolved at the site at which they occurred.

Managing Change and Innovation

Most people would probably identify some communication issue among the top three problems faced by individuals within the organization for which they work. This is not surprising. Communication problems are part of the human condition. Individuals often do not hear what the other person is saying because they do not see what the other person is seeing. Good communication is dependent upon the ability to perceive what the other person or group sees, as noted earlier in the chapter.

An increasingly popular technique for avoiding problems before they start is the use of *vertical teams* when a district is beginning a program initiative or studying a problem, especially if a district has not moved very far toward a site-based decision-making model. In a vertical team, representatives from all of the levels in the organization participate in fashioning a plan or a solution.

Too often, teachers and even building administrators have been frustrated and demoralized when, after studying a issue, whether curriculum initiative or building-level problem, they have forwarded a recommendation to the superintendent's office and found that it is ignored or so radically changed that it is unrecognizable. This often happens because central office staff see the problem from a different perspective or have information that was not available to the committee. Representatives of the superintendent and any other departments that will have a role in implementing a proposed decision should be at the table as a decision is fashioned. Thus all relevant information is available to everyone at the start of deliberations, and all perceptions can be accounted for as the decision is being formed.

Obviously, there is only one superintendent in each district and often only one individual responsible for each major function in many districts. No office would be capable of participating in a variety of committees. But that is not necessary. Including the appropriate individual(s) at the initial meeting to obtain commitment to the project and inviting these individuals to meetings at important decision points along the way, as well as providing copies of all meeting minutes, will make possible real participation by central office staff in the work of the committee.

Standing Committees

The fastest growing technique for maintaining a win/win attitude in a school district and dealing with issues before they escalate into major problems in the next round of negotiations is the establishment of a standing committee. The standing committee consists of teachers, building-level administrators, central office administrators, and, where feasible and consistent with local culture, board members who review problem issues apart from the formal grievance procedure and make changes in operations and, if necessary, the contract, when problems arise that were unforeseen by both parties during negotiations. The notion that a contract, once signed, should never be changed, no matter how serious a problem may develop as a result of changed or unforeseen circumstances, is an idea that is being seriously reconsidered by those interested in a partnership in which the well-being of students, the satisfaction of staff, and the success of the district are the primary goals of both parties.

Summary

It is an imperfect world. No matter how enlightened or progressive the intentions of both parties, conflicts will arise. Problems may present themselves in the process of negotiating a contract or living with it. Accepting these inevitabilities as challenges to be overcome in a total relationship permits candid discussion about how difficulties can be resolved by the parties themselves, even though outside assistance may be requested. The need to resolve emerging issues does not, by itself, make for a flawed relationship. It is the failure to anticipate and strategize methods for dealing with problems that can create a fundamental weakness in the foundation of the partnership. Even conventional dispute resolution techniques can be reinvented to solve problems and strengthen the relationship between the board, administration, and staff.

5

Collective Bargaining in the Future

Moving toward professional unionism involves the pain of un-learning old values and behaviors and the discomfort of working in ambiguous situations where the division of authority is un-clear and solutions to the problems are largely unknown. Only desperate people will do this.

J. E. Koppich (Koppich, 1993, p. 196)

Teachers' salaries have improved significantly since the 1960s. A few teachers in the United States are making more than $60,000 for a regular school year. Several states, such as Tennessee and Mississippi, made improvement of teacher salaries a fundamental part of their school reform efforts. Although teachers may worry about keeping the gains they have made, many are satisfied that they have achieved a fair place in the compensation hierarchy. Bargaining for economics in many instances is bargaining to maintain the present standard of living. Few school board members or legislators can quarrel seriously with that goal. It is almost certainly one they hold out for themselves in their own work environments. The noxious gas of confrontation on this topic may be blowing out of the window of the negotiating room.

Profound shifts in thinking about the psychology of workers and the appropriate ways to organize the workplace are having an even greater impact on contemporary bargaining theory. Concepts that are fundamentally different from those that pertained during the early days of collective bargaining are driving the American workplace in the 1990s. Today, employers look for workers who are self-motivated problem solvers. They solicit ideas and suggestions from workers. Even the relatively restricted efforts of Quality Circle techniques to elicit the ideas of employees within the narrow range of their assigned jobs have been found inadequate. Companies seek to get worker commitment to the company vision and seek out worker ideas on a whole host of corporate issues through vertical teams and focus group problem-solving sessions. Today, the worker is necessarily in control of the work environment if quality products are to be produced.

Education has not remained immune to these changes. Collective bargaining must change and is changing.

Will Unions and Bargaining Disappear?

It is no more likely that unionism and bargaining will disappear from the education industry than from the private sector. A new generation of leaders is coming to power in many of the industrial unions. Many are promising to renew recruiting efforts that have been largely ignored in the past several decades.

Unions have served two basic functions on behalf of workers in the 20th century: ensuring due process rights and speaking for workers when the resources of the enterprise are apportioned. Money, time, space, and facilities are all resources that directly affect compensation and working conditions. As long as school districts operate within a public political context, and that is likely to be a very long time, teachers will want assurance of fair treatment by boards of education and their administrators. This is especially true when tenure is under attack in many states as a redundant form of due process because many teachers have contractual due-process protections. Ironically, attempts to remove "fair share" or "agency shop" provisions of current contracts also contribute to teacher apprehensions and will foster the continuing existence of unions.

By its very definition, a partnership implies two or more independent entities coming together for the mutual benefit of the parties. Independent unions, serving as a unified voice for the teaching staff, are therefore likely to remain the mechanism of choice for ensuring teachers the right to be heard on issues of importance to them.

Will Union-Board Relationships Change?

A partnership cannot survive in constant conflict and turmoil. As has been argued throughout this book, the very entity that gives a reason for existence to unions and boards of education—public education—cannot survive, certainly not in a vigorous and healthy manner, if there is not a constant movement forward in the ability of labor and management to cooperate.

Harbison and Coleman (1951) suggested that four major stages in the relationship between boards and unions in the bargaining process can be described: pure confrontation, armed truce, working harmony, and true partnership.

It is ironic that a frequent precursor to an interest in cooperative bargaining has been a first-stage relationship between the parties: pure confrontation. Only parties who have lived in this zone for a while see the absolute futility of continuing such a relationship.

A state of armed truce between the parties may keep them out of the newspapers, but there are few other benefits. Suspicion, mistrust, game playing, challenging, blaming, and power politics are all part of the continuing interactions between the parties. The best resolution that can be hoped for in dealing with differences is a compromise, a course of action that both parties may grudgingly accept though neither prefers—the virtual equivalent of a "lose/lose" situation.

The only viable relationships that can support a healthy future are working harmony and true partnership. Working harmony may best describe the relationship that has existed in school districts that have functioned successfully in a traditional bargaining mode. Both sides appreciate the contributions of the other to the success of the district. Difficult problems are analyzed fully, and options for resolution are carefully considered. Even compromise solutions are cheerfully accepted because so much effort has gone into understanding the other side's problems.

Nevertheless, the traditional bargaining game is played with the roles, rules, and relationships that have prevailed since collective bargaining started. The board makes policies; teachers carry them out. Principals are the leaders, teachers the followers. This may not be how the system really works, but everyone pretends that it is because it is too exhausting to challenge whether a new approach is needed or has, in fact, begun to operate.

Only the true partnership will meet the needs of the future. Only someone who knows nothing about the daily operation of education can believe that principals "control" how teachers operate in the classroom. Only the totally uninitiated can believe that a school can be successful as a result of the autonomous actions of teachers acting in their classrooms independent of other teachers in the building. Only someone who has not yet studied the situation closely can believe that school boards and unions can fight over policy, curriculum, and student learning results and also maximize learning opportunities for children and adults.

True partnership is necessary because of the interrelationship of actions required to achieve organizational goals, not because the idea is trendy. General Motors, Chrysler, and Ford cannot bring a quality car off the production line, no matter how brilliant their chief executives, without the willing commitment of workers to build and assemble such a car every minute of every day. It is even less likely that the intellectual, psychic, and physical capabilities of children can be developed to the maximum extent possible without a total team effort.

Board-union relationships will change in those environments where necessary because dysfunction is the best that can be hoped for if they do not; a debacle for everyone is the more likely result.

But the modern world is not perfect. Progress toward partnership will not, in many instances, be a straight-line journey. All relationships are dynamic. A husband may love his wife dearly, but every minute of every day in their relationship is not pure bliss. Parents may love their children beyond life itself, but some days, months, even years, especially teenage years, can be challenging and often conflict laden. The basic relationship survives these

Figure 5.1 Flow of the Union-Board Relationship Over Time

storms because the parties see themselves as inevitably and inextricably intertwined. They are more complete with the relationship than without it.

Board-union relationships of the future will be dynamic, just as they have been in the past. As always, a change in personalities within the relationship may affect the partnership significantly. A school board or union election may change the nature of interaction between the parties for better or worse. However, to the extent that the body politic on both sides understands the importance of an enduring quality relationship, setbacks can be temporary. Figure 5.1 suggests the natural peaks and valleys that occur in the relationship between unions and school boards.

Changing Roles, Changing Relationships

The Changing Role of Teachers

One recent publication on negotiations in the education sector (Geisert & Lieberman, 1994) views cooperative bargaining as largely a bad deal for school boards. The authors view the issue of "empowerment" as a tradeoff in which the school board gives up its managerial prerogatives in return for a "less adversarial" relationship. This view represents unadulterated traditional thinking. In today's public attitude of dissatisfaction with schools, it is probably the teachers who have a greater need for a less adversarial relationship than the largely invisible board of education. In the many volumes of research about how to improve schools, it is the managerial decisions of teachers about how to use time, technology, community experts, and other resources that affect the achievement of students more than almost any resource-allocation decision the board of education might make.

Significant changes are taking place in the role of teachers that have their roots in research and confirmed practice, not in unproved theory. Teachers individually and collectively as a faculty are taking more responsibility for curriculum, instruction, and student success. These changes have their counterparts in private industry, where decision making is being decentralized. Such shifts in responsibility are occurring all over for the same reasons: Research and experience both show that such changes are necessary.

The Changing Role of Administrators

The proliferation of knowledge that teachers must master to do their jobs, from space science to AIDS; the many new technologies they must learn in order to create a modern learning environment; and the growing diversity of cultures and languages in the classroom with which they must cope make it inconceivable that superintendents can mandate the "best" way to teach or that principals can be expected by themselves to model exemplary teaching in the classroom.

Superintendents can work with their board and community to create a vision for the district and target key goals for education, goals that define some of the content of the curriculum and the opportunities that will be available to students in the classroom, from small class size to technology resources. They can join with the board in educating the public about the challenges that the district faces and the resources necessary to meet these challenges. But they cannot effectively tell teachers how to make all learners successful.

Principals can help interpret a district vision to the school's patrons and work with parents, staff, and other citizens to create one for their own school. They can foster a new culture of collaboration and search for best practice among staff. But they cannot be expected to tell individual teachers how to be successful, although they can occasionally help them when they are not succeeding or ensure opportunities for continuing development that will make each of them more effective practitioners. They can live the leadership paradox: encouraging each staff member to be responsible, promoting the responsibility of the total faculty for the quality of the school, and accepting personal responsibility for results. They can provide feedback. They can collect data about the effectiveness of the school, but they cannot hope to do alone what only teachers can do working alone and together.

Organizational and Cultural Change

Schools are experiencing an emerging change in school organization. This change is driven by and results in changes in school culture. For example, second-grade teachers are realizing that their success is dependent on the work of the teachers who instructed their students the prior year. If they want to take responsibility for the output at the end of their year of instruction, they need to take some responsibility for the input, the learning of students who will enter their classes at the beginning of the year. Thus teachers are joining together to plan for and sometimes share responsibility for groups of students. This may take the form of a primary unit cohort of teachers, each agreeing to pick up a group of students in kindergarten or first grade and instruct these students for 2 or 3 years, through the third grade. Or it might mean a group of teachers creating a semidepartmentalized organization in which one teacher instructs all second graders in science and another instructs all second graders in math, and so forth.

The way teachers decide to instruct students represents an organizational change. The willingness of a group of teachers to plan together for more than one class of students represents a change in a traditional cultural norm: blind obedience to the concept of the autonomy of individual teachers. Perhaps an even more profound culture shift can be seen in the joint acceptance of responsibility for student learning. Accountability for results is moving from an obligation imposed on teachers by the school board to a self-imposed requirement. The former practice effort gave rise to all kinds of

haggling at the bargaining table over supervision practices, evalu-
ation documents, and a myriad of other issues designed to get
teachers to "perform." In addition, the norm of continuous improvement based on data feedback is being established. Data goes
from being individually owned by the classroom teacher to being
owned by the staff. Tomorrow's instruction can be better than today's because staffs are searching for tools and techniques that can
be shown to make a difference.

Much has been made of the concept of site-based decision
making. This is also no theoretical construct to be adopted by be-
neficent school boards and their administrations. It is another ac-
knowledgment that some decisions must be made closest to the
point of delivery of a function or service because people at that site
are in the best position to understand all relevant information necessary to make good decisions. Middle managers are disappearing
from the corporate world because in the "second wave," middle
managers made decisions based on information they had that
workers needed. Computers now make it possible to move all necessary information right to the elbow of the worker.

This is true in schools as well. Teachers who live with and ob-
serve students every day and who talk with parents and guardians
frequently are, if properly trained, the appropriate people to make
critical decisions about how to deliver the educational program.
They are in the best position, if they have appropriate feedback
about the effects of their work, to decide how to allocate the resources of time, space, and materials to improve student learning.

Future Changes in the Collective Bargaining Process

Perhaps the most hopeful sign of a new generation of bargaining can be found in the descriptions of probable future changes
that have been outlined by scholars who have studied collective
bargaining in education and by leaders of the National Education
Association (NEA, 1993), the largest teachers union in America by
far. Their congruence of opinion offers to present practitioners of
collective bargaining a road map of how to get to a win/win future.
Four trends have been identified by many who have looked to the
future of bargaining.

1. Policy issues will be brought to the bargaining table. Perhaps the most often repeated shibboleth of school district governance is the notion that policy issues belong to the board alone and are not to be touched by administration, including superintendents, or teachers, and certainly not unions. Of course, prior to collective bargaining, some of the most important policy decisions made by boards of education related to staff compensation and working conditions. So bargaining itself started by dealing with policy issues, and union officials never stopped trying to enlarge the scope of policy issues that could be considered a working condition under state law or that the board could be cajoled into discussing in the bargaining process irrespective of state law.

Most thoughtful commentators argue that policy issues necessarily will become part of the bargaining process because policies drive so many issues related to instruction; for example, policies related to curriculum adoption, budget allocations, and school schedules. The goal of such discussions would not be to take a prerogative away from the board but to recognize that more flexibility may be needed in designing learning experiences for students than may be possible under "one-size-fits-all" district policies. A more complete process to ensure that the board hears the viewpoint of teachers when dealing with policy adoptions or changes is necessary.

2. The distinction between managers and workers will be reconsidered. Principals are trained today to accept the notion that leadership is not primarily a condition of an office or the perquisite of a title. Leadership is a force that is everywhere if the principal knows how to harness it. Principals are most appropriately described as leaders of leaders. Their primary role is to find the leadership potential in everyone and allow that potential to grow and flourish.

In addition, as pointed out elsewhere in this chapter, schools are moving from a concept of administrative accountability to staff accountability. If a school fails, it may not be because the principal is ineffective, although that will always remain a possibility. It may also be the result of a staff that has not worked together effectively to carry out its joint responsibility.

Managers are classically defined as individuals who plan activities, adjust work schedules, and evaluate the results of these managerial efforts. But if the classroom and school are, in fact, the locus of change, the teacher is more the manager than the principal. Trying to make a distinction between a principal and a teacher as a manager tells us nothing important about how schools work and actually confuses the issue.

3. *Formal bargaining will deal with limited issues.* The formal collective bargaining process will be limited to "bread-and-butter" issues, such as wages, and macro-working-condition issues, such as the number of required days of service. In addition, bargainers will identify "structures and ground rules" for staff involvement in dealing with educational issues that confront the district and individual buildings. Standing and ad hoc committees will deal with these issues in a consensus decision-making model. More permanent decisions can be formalized in separate written statements or agreements with their own duration. In California, such documents are called Education Policy Trust Agreements. Another approach to establishing the duration of such agreements is to "sunset" them after a period of time. When the agreement expires, the parties can decide whether to renew them as written, modify them, or abandon them.

4. *Master contracts and board policies will be subject to change when needed.* Wise negotiators working in a conventional bargaining mode like nothing better than a "zipper clause" in the master contract. This assures them that no subject not contained in the contract can become an issue of debate during the period that the master contract is in force. In effect, they view this as a tool to ensure their management prerogatives during the term of the contract. This makes sense if you are dealing with an antagonist. Getting the antagonist "out of your hair" for several years seems idyllic.

However, if both parties are involved in a partnership, their joint goal is to make the partnership successful. If a problem arises, no matter the source of the problem, it must be addressed; this includes unforeseen problems that arise out of contract language or board policy language.

Getting Started

If it is contended that a cooperative approach to collective bargaining is the necessary direction for the future, the reader might ask why this tool was not used in some of the more recent high-profile labor relations struggles, such as the major league baseball strike. The answers are obvious.

Cooperative bargaining will work only when the parties are convinced separately that their best interests are served by helping the other party reach its own goals. There is no reason for either party to come to the table to engage in cooperative bargaining if other strategies, even highly confrontational postures, are more likely to achieve either party's interests. When the National Basketball Association was in a state of near collapse more than a decade ago, players and owners realized that they would all lose money unless they could find a way to survive, and thrive, together. They reached an agreement that enables basketball players to become rich beyond their dreams and has made the value of basketball franchises skyrocket. Baseball players and owners were not convinced that their best interests were achieved by working with the other party. The baseball negotiation became a crystal-clear example of a mutually destructive attempt by both parties to solve a problem by power.

Until recently, economic incentives to collaboration in education were, at best, unclear. Now that the financial security of public education seems more in jeopardy than ever before, the motivation is significant for boards of education and their administrations to reach out to education labor unions, most particularly teacher unions, with offers of a partnership relationship. The unions ought to respond quickly and positively if, in fact, they are not the ones who make the overture. There seems no other choice.

There is another difference between a business like baseball, part of the entertainment industry, and education. People enter education, to a greater or lesser extent, for altruistic reasons. Teachers, administrators, and board members are in the business of educating children because doing so is socially valuable and because it is emotionally and spiritually rewarding to them. To a very large extent, they share highly principled goals. *Only* by working together can they meet their highest needs for self-actualization.

Now is the time to initiate the partnership if one does not already exist. The public is watching.

Summary

More and more political leaders, responding to a prevailing business and public dissatisfaction with public education, have concluded that alternatives must be found for public schools as we know them. This growing sentiment is so widespread that university scholars and unions themselves have begun to ask fundamental questions about the place of collective bargaining in an education environment growing more diverse by the day through voucher systems, charter schools, and other efforts to "break the monopoly of public education." They are reaching similar conclusions about how bargaining must evolve to permit schools and school districts to become more creative, innovative, and flexible. Bargaining must permit teaching to become a profession in the classic meaning of the term. Unions must broaden their focus to include substantive issues of school improvement if they are to appropriately serve the needs of education in the next century.

Resource A

Win/Win Bargaining:
A Practitioner's Checklist

A review of the following questions may be helpful in fostering a completion of the negotiations process that is satisfactory to both parties.

Task	Yes	No

Preparing to Bargain

Task	Yes	No
Has the rationale for win/win bargaining been accepted?	___	___
Will the board be directly involved? How?	___	___
Will the superintendent participate in discussions?	___	___
Has the role of principals in the process been clarified?	___	___
Has a prebargaining training program been designed?	___	___
Will the board and union train together?	___	___
Has a training leader been identified?	___	___
Have constituents been prepared for win/win bargaining?	___	___
Is there constituent support for win/win bargaining?	___	___
Has a plan been designed to keep constituents informed during negotiations?	___	___

Task	Yes	No

Conducting Bargaining

Have ground rules for meetings been adopted? ___ ___
Have leadership roles been clarified? ___ ___
Do both parties accept consensus decision making? ___ ___
Do both parties share a common definition of
consensus? ___ ___
Have the parties planned how to handle press
relations? ___ ___
Has a process for ongoing communication with
constituents been defined? ___ ___
Has a process been identified for each party to
present its issues at the table? ___ ___
Will both sides have the opportunity to offer
solutions to identified problems? ___ ___
Are brainstorming activities a regular part of
problem solving? ___ ___
Has all necessary information been made available
to the other group? ___ ___
Have objective criteria been required in presenting
proposed solutions to problems? ___ ___

Resolving Current Conflicts

Have difficult issues been thoroughly analyzed
from the other's point of view? ___ ___
Is problem solving halted only because a matter of
principle is now involved? ___ ___
Is the other party unable to move further because
of a fundamental principle? ___ ___
Have other districts found ways to deal with this
principle conflict? ___ ___
Has the use of one or more third parties been
considered as a way to mediate a dispute? ___ ___

Task	Yes	No

Preventing Future Problems

Has staff been adequately trained regarding the
intent of each article of the signed contract?   ___ ___

Have committees been created for dealing with
new initiatives or problems?   ___ ___

Do these committees ensure input from all levels
of the organization during the study?   ___ ___

Does each party periodically review its commitment
to win/win bargaining?   ___ ___

Is the district making progress toward more faculty
collaboration at each school?   ___ ___

Are building administrators and faculty working
as a team rather than a hierarchy?   ___ ___

Is the leadership potential of each staff member
nurtured?   ___ ___

Are policy and contract language impediments to
school improvement open to prompt consideration
and change?   ___ ___

Glossary

Collective bargaining in public education is more likely to be redesigned effectively if all of those engaged in conversation about how to improve its functioning have a common understanding of several key terms that appear throughout the literature. Some of these terms, as noted below, are not always used synonymously by all writers. This list is very limited, focused basically on important terms used in this book.

Agency shop: An employee, as a condition of employment, must either join the recognized or certified employee organization or pay the organization a service fee for bargaining services. Considerable litigation has occurred recently as to how much of the total amount of dues paid by members can be considered fees for bargaining services, also known as *fair share* in some states.

Collaborative bargaining: An expression used by many but not all writers to refer to a form of bargaining in which both parties collaborate to solve problems that each side brings to the table. This is sometimes referred to as *win/win bargaining*. The effort is to find final solutions that both parties can accept, and thereby "win." See **Principled bargaining** below.

Collective bargaining: A legally defined process whereby representatives of workers and management meet to develop a written contract. Bargainable issues are prescribed by law in the public sector, often subsumed under the general topics of wages, hours, and working conditions. This process is a category of the broader term *negotiations.*

Distributive bargaining: A term that refers to the traditional concept of collective bargaining, which is considered to be a "zero-sum" game. For every gain achieved by labor, management is deemed to have lost something, whether power or authority or resources. Also called *win/lose bargaining.*

Expedited bargaining: The negotiating parties agree to reach agreement in a defined short period of time and limit the number of issues that can be brought to the table. If agreement is not reached within the self-imposed time limit, the parties proceed to the regular bargaining process.

Integrative bargaining: A term that is sometimes used synonymously for **Collaborative bargaining.** Discussions are focused not on positions but on shared or common problems and interests of each side. Both parties work together to find solutions satisfactory to both; for example, a salary increase that will protect workers against inflation and the employer against financial difficulty.

Management rights clause: Language in the agreement that reserves certain rights to management that are not subject to the grievance procedure or arbitration.

Negotiations: Any process during which individuals or groups come together to reconcile needs or interests. Transactions between purchasers and sellers, sovereign nations seeking a treaty, and an adolescent and a parent seeking to define a curfew hour all can be considered negotiation. Publications about this topic often deal with a broad interpretation of the word.

Principled bargaining: A term used by Fisher and Ury (1981) to distinguish it from collaborative bargaining, which they view as a misleading expression; it can suggest that either side must give up important interests for the sake of pleasant relations between the parties. Principled negotiations are focused on the important interests of each party, not any particular table position. Both sides seek to reach a mutually satisfactory agreement without abandoning key interests.

Strategic bargaining: Each party develops a projection of the organization's future. Projections are reconciled, and goals are established. Joint committees study each area and then negotiate toward preestablished goals.

Work to rule: Union members carry out only those work responsibilities that are addressed in the master contract and only at a level mandated by the contract; for example, if teachers are required to be in their classrooms 15 minutes before students arrive, teachers will not enter the building until exactly 15 minutes before doors are opened to students.

Zipper clause: A contract provision that prevents further bargaining during the term of the agreement.

Annotated Bibliography, Other Suggested Readings, and References

Annotated Bibliography

The following citations contain information that will be helpful not only to those responsible for negotating a contract but also to those who seek further understanding of the process in light of the rapidly changing circumstances under which public educaton is operating. This information might be especially helpful to building principals who have first-line responsibility for implementing a contract within an environment of changing public attitudes and teacher expectations.

Cohen-Rosenthal, E., & Burton, C. E. (1987). *Mutual gains: A guide to union-management cooperation.* New York: Praeger.

Although written to guide labor management relations in private enterprise, this book contains particularly valuable sections on the risks as well as the benefits of cooperation, the initial steps necessary to create a productive relationship, and practical suggestions for negotiating procedures and grievance handling as joint problem-solving experiences.

Eberts, R., & Stone, J. A. (1984). *The effects of collective bargaining on American education.* Lexington, MA: Lexington Books.

This is an account of a 4-year study of the effects of collective bargaining. Although somewhat dated now, it illustrates why some educators will be reluctant to move to a new paradigm of collective bargaining. Data presented here show that teachers covered by collective bargaining agreements (negotiated before the newer approaches to bargaining became popular) receive higher salaries, teach smaller classes, and spend slightly more time instructing students but more time preparing for classes than do their colleagues who are not covered by collective bargaining laws.

Fisher, R., & Ury, W. (1981). *Getting to yes: Negotiating agreement without giving in* (2nd ed.). Boston: Houghton Mifflin.

This publication had significant impact in creating interest in "win/win" bargaining. The driving concept is "principled negotiation," a process whereby both parties attempt to decide issues on their merits rather than engage in stale rituals of haggling over "positions" and "throw-away" issues. The goal is mutual gain for both parties. When "interests" conflict, both parties search for fair and independent standards that can guide a resolution of the dispute. It takes a realistic view of collective bargaining, admitting that not all parties will walk down this road. Therefore, negotiators must prepare their BATNA—best alternative to a negotiated agreement—if problems cannot be resolved. This book was revised with a third author, B. Patton, in a 1991 edition published by Penguin Books, but this revised version is not always easy to find.

Geisert, G., & Lieberman, M. (1994). *Teacher union bargaining: Practice and policy.* Chicago: Precept Press.

This book is predicated on a conventional concept of collective bargaining as inherently and inevitably adversarial. Concepts such as win/win negotations, empowerment, and site-based management are portrayed as muddle-headed thinking on the part of administrators. The authors feel that such ideas merely present opportunities for unions to build their influence and reduce administration's ability to *manage on behalf of the community. Part 1 deals with bargaining tactics. Part 2 analyzes policy issues such as strikes, compulsory binding arbitration, and alternatives to collective bargaining for public employees.*

Herman, J. J., & Megiveron, G. (1993). *Collective bargaining in education: Win/win. Win/lose. Lose/lose.* Lancaster, PA: Technomic.

This text does a better job than most in portraying the rubrics of traditional collective bargaining within the context of major new initiatives in education, such as teacher empowerment and site-based decision making. It gives a fair-minded summary of the strengths and weaknesses of win/win bargaining as the primary approach to getting a master agreement.

Kerchner, C. T., & Koppich, J. E. (Eds.). (1993). *A union of professionals: Labor relations and educational reform.* New York: Teachers College Press.

An excellent effort to capture the fundamental changes taking place in bargaining relationships between education management and teacher unions, and to document successes and failures. The premise of the book is that some unions are trying to graft professional values onto the traditional principles and practices of industrial unionism and to balance the need to protect individual needs and interests of teachers with the goal of ensuring the quality and integrity of teaching and the viability of public education. Nine case studies of efforts to achieve school reform through changes in management-union relations and collective bargaining are analyzed.

Kerchner, C. T., & Mitchell, D. (1988). *The changing idea of a teacher's union.* Philadelphia: Falmer.

This book offers its own version of the "third wave": The authors describe three generations of teacher organizations. The first refers to the period in which teachers were organized, at least loosely, but had, at best, only the right to meet and confer with their employers. The second generation covers the period of industrial-style collective bargaining. The third generation will be a period dominated by what the authors call "professional unions." This period will be driven by the shifting of power away from a central decision-making point (a trend affecting both private and public organizations), the need to change the culture of schools toward shared values and mutual planning, and the shared responsibility for the success of the school in response to the public's insistence on results.

Lewicki, R. J., Litterer, J. A., Saunders, D. M., & Minton, J. W. (1993). *Negotiation: Readings, exercises and cases* (2nd ed.). Burr Ridge, IL: Irwin.

A so-called readings book that accompanies a textbook by the same name and runs parallel to it in structure. However, for the general reader trying to understand the major strategies and issues in negotiation—including, but not limited to, collective bargaining—this book is ideal. Fourteen sections (such as "Interdependence," "Distributive Bargaining: Strategy and Tactics," "Integrative Bargaining," "Negotiation Breakdown: Causes and Cures," and "Ethics") begin with an introductory page identifying the key elements of a topic and are followed by a series of five- to nine-page readings on the general subject. More serious readers can pursue the cases and exercises at the end of the book.

National Education Association. (1991). *Collaborative bargaining: A critical appraisal.* Washington, DC: National Education Association Research Division.

This 52-page softcover book, part of the NEA's "Studies in Collective Bargaining" series, analyzes the social forces that precipitated interest in collaborative bargaining, discusses the work of some of the major proponents of new approaches to collective bargaining (Irving Goldaber's win/win, Fisher and Ury's principled bargaining, Cohen-Rosenthal and Burton's strategic bargaining), and summarizes some of the potential benefits and problems of collaborative bargaining.

National Education Association. (1992). *Negotiating change: Education reform and collective bargaining.* Washington, DC: National Education Association Research Division.

Another volume in NEA's "Studies in Collective Bargaining" series, this publication lays out a theoretical framework for the NEA's inter-

est in using the collective bargaining process as a means for attaining permanent school district reform. Authors note that, as of the date of the publication, 34 states and the District of Columbia have collective bargaining statutes covering public school teachers. Several of these laws strictly limit the areas of collective bargaining. Nevertheless, the publication argues that some of the policy issues related to reform are so inextricably tied to issues of "hours, wages, and working conditions" that negotiated agreements on many of these issues will help managers by "institutionalizing district policy" and thereby ensuring teacher support. The text shows how such matters can be "negotiated" even in states that lack official sanction for collective bargaining.

National Education Association. (1993). *Advancing the national education goals: The role of collective bargaining.* Washington, DC: National Education Association Research Division.

This book, the third in 3 years by the NEA that attempts to explain the organization's position on collective bargaining at a time of school reform, may be the best. It is actually a selection of addresses delivered to the NEA national conference in March 1992. NEA general counsel Robert Chernin's description of new directions for schools and bargaining is the most revealing document in the collection and is consistent with many of the changes being predicted by some scholars: the movement of policy issues to the bargaining table, a blurring of the distinctions between administrators and teachers, the limitation of master contracts to fundamental issues such as wages and working conditions, and the development of "structures and ground rules" for year-round discussion of educational issues apart from the bargaining process.

Woodworth, W. P., & Meek, C. B. (1995). *Creating labor-management partnerships.* Reading, MA: Addison-Wesley.

One of the many recent books that calls for labor-management collaboration so that companies can function competitively and therefore successfully in an economy increasingly based on global competition. The book defines the roles, rules, and procedures necessary for a successful partnership; offers suggestions for avoiding intraorganization political turmoil as relationships move from old models to new ones; and suggests examples of defined problem-solving initiatives that can lead to changing the broader organizational culture. Efforts at cooperative problem solving are conducted parallel to, not in place of, collective bargaining. Although the book looks at a private industry environment, the theory and processes suggested have application to education.

Wynn, R. (1983). *Collective bargaining: An alternative to conventional bargaining.* Indianapolis, IN: Phi Delta Kappa Educational Foundation.

This is one of the earliest and most influential publications in the educational literature regarding what became known popularly as win/win bargaining. This short monograph quickly summarizes the philosophical underpinnings of this new concept of bargaining and supplies two case studies of districts trying to resolve issues by discussing mutual perceptions of problems rather than arguing over positions. In the first case study, Wynn describes an ongoing approach to problem solving in an Illinois school district. The other case study demonstrates the "communication laboratory" approach to bargaining promoted by the late Irving Goldaber.

Other Suggested Readings

Hendrickson, G. (1990). Where do you go after you get to yes? *The Executive Educator, 12,* 16-17.

Herman, J. J. (1991). The two faces of collective bargaining. *School Business Affairs, 57,* 10-13.

Huang, W., (Ed.). (1989). *Organized labor at the crossroads.* Kalamazoo, MI: Upjohn Institute for Employment Research.

Johnson, S. M. (1987). Can schools be reformed at the bargaining table? *Teachers College Record, 89,* 269-280.

Lax, D. A., & Sebanius, J. K. (1993). Interests: The measure of negotiation. In R. J. Lewicki, J. A. Litterer, J. W. Minton, & D. M. Saunders (Eds.), *Negotiation: Readings, exercises, cases* (2nd ed., pp. 130-150). Burr Ridge, IL: Irwin.

Lippitt, G. L. (1983). Can conflict resolution be win/win? *The School Administrator, 40,* 20-21.

Many, T. W., & Sloan, C. A. (1990). Management and labor perceptions of school collective bargaining. *Journal of Collective Negotiations in the Public Sector, 19,* 283-296.

Thompson, B. L. (1991). Negotiations training: Win/win or what? *Training, 26,* 31-35.

Troy, L. (1986). The rise and fall of American trade unions: The labor movement from FDR to RR. In S. M. Lipsit (Ed.), *Unions in transition: Entering the second century* (pp. 75-109). San Francisco: ICS Press.

Ury, W. L., Brett, J. M., & Goldberg, S. (1988). *Getting disputes resolved: Designing systems to cut the cost of conflict.* San Francisco: Jossey-Bass.

References

Allman, W. F. (1984). Nice guys finish first: When dealing with your neighbor, a business rival, or the Soviet Union, the way to get ahead is to go along. *Science, 84*(5), 24-32.

Cohen-Rosenthal, E., & Burton, C.E. (1987). *Mutual gains: A guide to union-management cooperation.* New York: Prager.

Fisher, R., Kopelman, E., & Schneider, A. K. (1994). *Beyond Machiavelli: Tools for coping with conflict.* Cambridge, MA: Harvard University Press.

Fisher, R., & Ury, W. (1981). *Getting to yes: Negotiating agreement without giving in* (2nd ed.). Boston: Houghton Mifflin.

Geisert, G., & Lieberman, M. (1994). *Teacher union bargaining: Practice and policy.* Chicago: Precept Press.

Goldaber, I. (1982). *Transforming conflict into a win/win outcome.* Salem, OR: Confederation of Oregon School Administrators.

Harbison, F., & Coleman, J. R. (1951). *Goals and strategy in collective bargaining.* New York: Harper & Brothers.

Hess, G. A. (1991). *School restructuring, Chicago style.* Newbury Park, CA: Corwin.

Kerchner, C. T., & Koppich, J. E. (Eds.). (1993). *A union of professionals: Labor relations and educational reform.* New York: Teachers College Press.

Kohn, A. (1986). *No contest: The case against competition.* Boston: Houghton Mifflin.

Koppich, J. E. (1993). Getting started: A primer on professional unionism. In C. T. Kerchner & J. E. Koppich (Eds.), *A union of professionals: Labor relations and educational reform,* pp. 194-204. New York: Teachers College Press.

McGregor, D. (1960). *The human side of enterprise.* New York: McGraw-Hill.

National Education Association. (1993). *Advancing the national educational goals: The role of collective bargaining.* Washington, DC: National Education Association Research Division.

Patterson, J. (1993). *Leadership for tomorrow's schools.* Alexandria, VA: Association for Supervision and Curriculum Development.

Senge, P. (1990). *The fifth discipline: The art and practice of the learning organization.* New York: Currency Doubleday.

Susskind, L., & Cruikshank, J. (1987). *Breaking the impasse: Consensual approaches to resolving public disputes.* New York: Basic Books.

Taylor, F. W. (1911). *The principles of scientific management.* New York: Harper & Row.

Twentieth Century Fund. (1992). *Facing the challenge: Report of the Twentieth Century Fund Task Force on School Governance.* New York: Author.

United States Commission on Excellence in Education. (1983). *A nation at risk: The imperative for educational reform.* Washington, DC: U.S. Superintendent of Documents.

Usdan, M.D., Kirst, M. W., & Danzberger, J. (1992). *Governing the public schools: New times, new requirements.* Washington, DC: Institute for Educational Leadership.

Woodworth, W. P., & Meek, C. B. (1995). *Creating labor-management partnerships.* Reading, MA: Addison-Wesley.